ALPHIE WOLFIE JR. & LUNA

WANT YOU TO
READ, LEAD, SUCCEED!
Donated by Wolf Pack Athletics
ONE COMMUNITY, ONE PACK

To the passionate and loyal fans of the Nevada Wolf Pack. – CLN / JTN

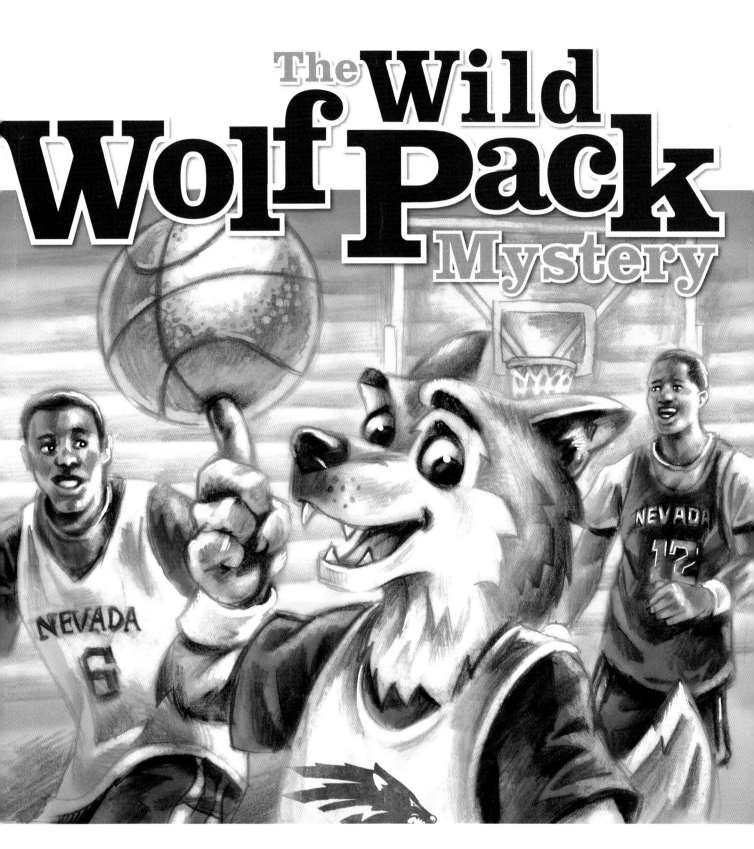

The Wild Wolf Pack Mystery

WRITTEN BY

Chris & Jennifer Newbold

ILLUSTRATED BY

Robert Rath

UNIVERSITY PRIDE PUBLISHING

GAME TIME!

"Tomorrow is
my big day,"
thought Alphie.

"I can hear it now – the thump of the basketball, the swish of the three-pointer, the shriek of the whistle, the blast of the buzzer!"

Alphie's fur tingled with excitement.

Tomorrow was the first Wolf Pack basketball game of the season.

He could hardly wait to see the silver and blue colors and the excited faces of little Wolf Pack fans!

"**I** must get ready
and pack my game bag.
The players are depending
on me," Alphie said.

"Let's see. What do I need to
bring with me to the game?"

"Camera – check!"

"Extra jersey – check!"

"Hula hoop – check!"

"Basketball – uh oh!"

"Where's the basketball?"

Alphie had always been the wolf in charge of the game day basketball.

The players trusted him to protect the ball until it was time to play.

Alphie had taken extra special care of the basketball since March, making sure it was properly inflated and stored safely in his cool, dark den.

"Oh where, oh where could that basketball be?" howled Alphie.

"It's not in my den! It's a mystery!"

"I must retrace my steps," Alphie
reasoned. "Certainly I can find it
if I just search hard enough.
Now, where was I yesterday?
I'll start by looking there first,"
he planned.

8

Thinking back, Alphie recalled that he started his morning with bird watching on Peavine Mountain.

"That's it! Maybe I left it near the 'N!'" he exclaimed.

Alphie Says

DID YOU KNOW?

The Nevada state bird is the Mountain Bluebird. It lives in the high country and its song is a clear, short warble like the caroling of a robin.

Alphie jumped on his mountain bike.

Huff, puff, huff, puff!
He pedaled hard up the mountain.

"Whew! Now where, oh where could that basketball be?" Alphie looked left and looked right, but there was no sign of it on the mountain.

Alphie Says **DID YOU KNOW?**
Peavine Mountain got its name from the wild, purple-flowered pea vine that grows near springs around the mountain. The highest point is 8,266 feet.

"Oh, dear," said Alphie, "I must move quickly
to find the ball in time for tomorrow's game!"

"What did I do next? After bird watching on
Peavine Mountain, I went snowboarding at Tahoe."

"That's it! Maybe I left it on
the ski hill!" thought Alphie.

Off Alphie sprinted, straight to the chairlift.

Shoosh, woosh, shoosh, woosh.
Alphie watched snowboarders and skiers carve tracks in the powder.

2

He checked high; he checked low.
There was no sign of the basketball around Tahoe.

Still retracing his steps
from the day before,
Alphie concentrated,
"Where did I go next?"

"Aha! I remember! All that snowboarding made me very
hungry, so I met Wolfie, Jr. on campus for a picnic lunch."

Alphie Says **DID YOU KNOW?**
The sculpture of John MacKay
on the Quad was created by
Gutzon Borglum, who also
sculpted Mount Rushmore.

"That's it! Maybe I left it on the Quad!"

Alphie raced to campus!

Chirp, chirp, tweet, tweet!
The birds sang playfully
in the trees.

"Whew! Now where,
oh where could that
basketball be?" asked
a puzzled Alphie.

Alphie Says DID YOU KNOW?

Great horned owl chicks roost
each spring in the trees that line
the Quad.

Alphie searched
the columns and
scoured the steps
of Morrill Hall.
There was no
sign of it on
the Quad.

Alphie was becoming very concerned. He was in charge of the basketball, and he couldn't find it anywhere!

How would the Wolf Pack play their game tomorrow without it? What would he tell the team? And what about all the little Wolf Pack fans?

He didn't want to let everyone down.

Alphie took a seat on the edge of Manzanita Lake to think hard about where he could have left the basketball.

Imagining yesterday's events, Alphie recalled, "After my picnic with Wolfie, Jr., I took my kayak out for an afternoon float. That's got to be it! Maybe I left it at the Truckee River Whitewater Park!"

Alphie Says DID YOU KNOW?

The Truckee River is thought to be named for a Paiute Chief. It is over 100 miles long and is home to a whitewater park with Class 2 and 3 rapids.

Alphie dashed to the river.

Splish, splash, splish, splash!
The cold water was rushing quickly.

"Whew! Now where, oh, where could that basketball be?" Alphie looked under the bridge and along the rocks.

There was no sign of it at the Truckee River.

21

Time was running out!

Alphie pictured the disappointed
faces of all the fans and wondered
what he should do.

"Maybe I could tell them the ball popped while I was riding my scooter," mused Alphie.

"Or maybe they'd believe me if I said I gave it away to a deserving little Wolf Pack fan," he schemed.

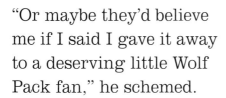

"I know! I could tell them a rebel stole the ball!"

After a few minutes thinking up all of the ways he could explain the missing basketball . . .

Alphie realized what he had to do. He must tell the players what really happened.

Sadly, Alphie shuffled toward the Lawlor Events Center.

The players were in the middle of practice, but as soon as they saw Alphie, they rushed to greet him.

They were thrilled to see their beloved wolf!

Alphie reluctantly shared the bad news. "Fellow Wolf Pack, I must report to you that somehow, somewhere, I lost the game day basketball you entrusted to me. I am very sorry and hope I can make it up to you."

26

"Hey, Alphie," yelled the point guard.
"Is this what you're looking for?"

Bouncing across the court came the game day basketball!

"I borrowed it yesterday for our practice. I must have forgotten to tell you," he said sheepishly.

Alphie leaped into the air! Hooray!
The mystery was solved!

He hadn't lost the basketball after all.

He couldn't wait to cheer on his
Wolf Pack at tomorrow's game!

The roar of the fans, the howls
of Wolfie, Jr., the chant of
"Law of the Jungle," the rim-rattle
of a dunk – he could hear it now . . .

The Law of the Jungle

Now this is "The Law of the Jungle"
– as old and as true as the sky;
And the Wolf that shall keep it may prosper,
but the Wolf that shall break it must die.
As the creeper that girdles the tree-trunk
the Law runneth forward and back —
For the strength of the Pack is the Wolf,
and the strength of the Wolf is the Pack.

Sing along to The **University** of **Nevada** fight song!

Hail to our sturdy team, loyal and true,
March! March on down that field, O' Silver and Blue!
We'll give a long cheer for Nevada's team.
See them break through again.
Fighting for our own U. of N. — to Victory!

(Repeat)

N!

E!

V!

A!

D!

A!

NEVADA!

We Want to Hear From You!

If your child, grandchild, niece, nephew, brother, sister or little wolf is a huge fan of *The Wild Wolf Pack Mystery*, let us know. Please visit our website at **www.universitypridepublishing.com** and share your story. If selected, your special Alphie fan will receive a handwritten note from the author and a special sketch from the illustrator, as well as limited edition bookmarks and coloring sheets inspired by the book. Go Wolf Pack!

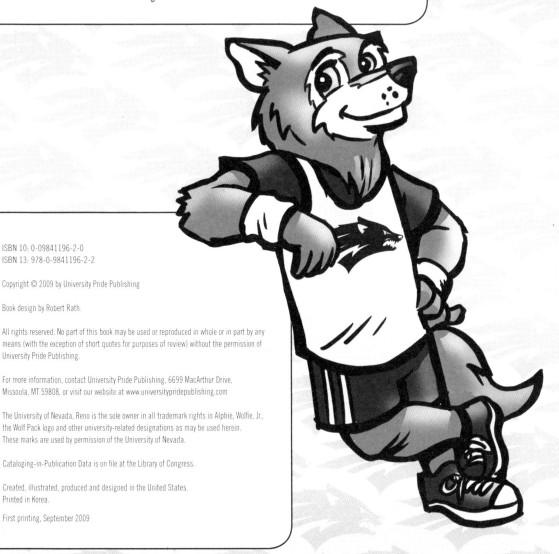

Many thanks and appreciation to those who helped bring
The Wild Wolf Pack Mystery to life (in alphabetical order):
Chris Fagan, Cade Kurtis Folgner, Susan L. Galbraith,
Donna Glogovac, David R. Grundy, Denise Lamb
and Darron J. Pinkney.

ISBN 10: 0-09841196-2-0
ISBN 13: 978-0-9841196-2-2

Copyright © 2009 by University Pride Publishing

Book design by Robert Rath.

For more information, contact University Pride Publishing, 6699 MacArthur Drive, Missoula, MT 59808, or visit our website at www.universitypridepublishing.com

The University of Nevada, Reno is the sole owner in all trademark rights in Alphie, Wolfie, Jr., the Wolf Pack logo and other university-related designations as may be used herein. These marks are used by permission of the University of Nevada.

Cataloging-in-Publication Data is on file at the Library of Congress.

Created, illustrated, produced and designed in the United States.
Printed in Korea.

First printing, September 2009